MW00624121

FAST, EASY, and TASTY
trail-tested recipes
for any outdoor activity

Origin Edition

by Chef Corso & the
MONTyBOCA community

TABLE OF CONTENTS

¡BUENO! Thanks for coming along!

Our mission at MONTyBOCA is to get folks excited about cooking outside!

Every recipe is trail-tested by a member of our community, and:

- uses 10 ingredients or less
- is ready in 30 min or less
- weighs as little as 8 oz for 2-4 servings
- requires no pre-prep, no dehydrating
- uses fresh, real ingredients
- is amazingly tasty!

We hope these meals fuel you and elevate your experience on your next epic thru hike or Sunday stroll.

**Get outside
Eat well
Share the tasty experience**

#elevateyourmeals

Cooking Checklist

- ☐ Stove - 2+ liter preferred for sharing
- ☐ Pot/pan
- ☐ Camping gas
- ☐ Lighter/matches
- ☐ Pocket knife or camp knife
- ☐ Serving bowls
- ☐ Utensils
- ☐ Mixing/packing container (try old coffee cans)
- ☐ Recipe
- ☐ FOOD!

Clothes Checklist

- [ ] Socks
- [ ] Undies
- [ ] Sports bra (if needed)
- [ ] T-shirt/tank
- [ ] Shirt, long sleeve
- [ ] Midlayer
- [ ] Rain jacket
- [ ] Vest
- [ ] Hat
- [ ] Beanie
- [ ] Bandeau/bandana
- [ ] Hair ties (if needed)
- [ ] Shorts
- [ ] Pants
- [ ] Swim suit
- [ ] Belt
- [ ] Small towel
- [ ] Hiking boots
- [ ] Clean change of clothes for the car

Equipment Checklist

A starting point for your trek.

- ☐ Backpack
- ☐ Tent
- ☐ Sleeping pad
- ☐ Sleeping bag
- ☐ Head lamp
- ☐ Head lamp batteries
- ☐ Rope for tying food away from critters
- ☐ Sunscreen
- ☐ Bug spray
- ☐ Extra caribiners
- ☐ First aid kit
- ☐ Water pump 1
- ☐ Water pump 2
- ☐ Water bottle(s)
- ☐ Hiking poles
- ☐ Camp stove
- ☐ Camp stove gas
- ☐ Pots/pan
- ☐ Lighter/matches
- ☐ Pocket knife/ Camp knife
- ☐ Serving bowls
- ☐ Utensils
- ☐ Recipes

MONT
Y BOCA

Breakfast

Brekkie Skillet w/ Chicken Sausage
San Dieo, CA

Dirtbag Eggs Benedict
Oakland, CA

Hula Brekkie Sliders
Honolulu, HI

Tropical Oatmeal
Chuckanut Drive, WA

Brekkie Skillet with Chicken Sausage

	Ingredients	US	Metrics
2 – 4 Servings			
	1. Water	32 oz	907 g
	2. Red potatoes	3-4	3-4
9 Ingredients	3. Salt	2 tsp	5 g
	4. Oil	2 TB	25 g
25 Minutes	5. Chicken sausage	12 oz	340 g
	6. Shallot	2	2
~5 lbs /	7. Red bell pepper	1	1
~2.2 kg Weight	8. Zucchini	2	2
	9. Fruit, seasonal fav	1-2	1-2

High Calorie

Dairy Free

Steps

1. CHOP potatoes into small chunks
2. **TURN ON BURNER. High heat**
3. + water, potatoes and 1 tsp salt to pot
4. BOIL until soft
5. while boiling, CHOP sausage, shallot, pepper, zucchini
6. DRAIN potatoes
7. + oil, shallot, sausage to potatoes
8. COOK 3-4 min. STIR
9. + pepper, zucchini, remaining salt
10. COOK 3-4 min until brown. STIR

EAT

Serve with your favorite cut fruit

Notes/Additions

Did you know that? Blood oranges originated in Sicily and Spain and varieties include Tarocco, Moro, and Sanguinello
Now you know!

Pack it out!

Dirtbag Eggs Benedict

2 – 4
Servings

9
Ingredients

20
Minutes

~2lbs
~1kg
Weight

`High Calorie`

`Low Water`

Ingredients

		US	Metrics
1.	English muffins	2-4	2-4
2.	Powdered eggs ◆	4 TB	40 g
3.	Water	6 oz	70 ml
4.	Ham	8-12 oz	325 g
5.	Hollandaise packet	1 (.9oz)	1 (25g)
6.	Oil	1/3 cup	50 g
7.	Salt	1/2 tsp	1 g
8.	Lemon	1	1
9.	Green onions	1/2 bunch	1/2 bunch

Steps

1. HYDRATE eggs with water. MIX. RESERVE
2. HYDRATE hollandaise packet with water, oil, squeeze of lemon, salt. RESERVE
3. SLICE english muffins
4. CHOP ham
5. **TURN BURNER ON: Med heat**
6. + oil. TOAST english muffins. RESERVE
7. + 1 TB oil, ham. COOK 2-3 min
8. + egg mixture. COOK 1-2. STIR
9. Push mixture to side of pan. In same pan, + hollandaise mixture
10. COOK, STIR 1-2 min until thick
11. ASSEMBLE

EAT

Pack it out!

Notes/Additions
Did you know that? Eggs Benedict was used as a hangover meal in the late 1800s? Now you know!

Coconut, Pineapple, Macadamia Nut Oatmeal

2
Servings

5
Ingredients

10
Minutes

~1.5 lbs / ~700 g
Weight

Vegan

Vegetarian

Dairy Free

Ingredients	US	Metrics
1. Coconut milk powder	3 TB	16 g
2. Water	16 oz	475 g
3. Instant oatmeal, plain	1 C	80 g
4. Dried pineapple	1/4 C	20 g
5. Macadamia nuts	1/4 C	20 g

Steps

1. **TURN ON BURNER: High heat**
2. + water, coconut milk powder
3. BOIL
4. CHOP pineapple, nuts
5. + oatmeal
6. SIMMER, STIR STIR 3-5 min until done
7. + pineapple, nuts
8. SIMMER 3 min. STIR STIR

EAT

Notes/Additions
Did you know that? The Macadamia was introduced into Hawaii around 1881 and only used ornamentally. Now you know!

Pack it out!

Hula Breakfast Sliders

2 – 4
Servings

5
Ingredients

20
Minutes

**~1.5 lbs /
~750 g**
Weight

High Calorie

Dairy Free

Low Water

Ingredients	US	Metrics
1. Water	4 TB	50 g
2. Powdered eggs	4 TB	40 g
3. Portuguese sausage	12 oz	340 g
4. Passion fruit jam	3 oz	85 g
5. Hawaiian slider rolls	8 (16 oz)	8

Steps

1. HYDRATE eggs. 5 min
2. SLICE sausage
3. **TURN BURNER ON: Med heat**
4. COOK sausage. 2-3 min. RESERVE. Save fat
5. COOK eggs in fat. 1-2 min
6. TOAST rolls
7. LAYER jam, sausage, eggs
EAT

Notes/Additions

*Did you know that? Passion Fruit is also known as
Lilikoil. Try some other jam or spreads to change it up.
Now you know!*

Pack it out!

14

Notes

Lunch

Kale Salad w/ Baby Tomatoes
North Cascades NP, WA

German Potato Salad
Port Angeles, WA

Moroccan Cous Cous
Joshua Tree NP, CA

Mediterranean Tuna
Central Park - NY, NY

Kale Salad w/ Shallot & Baby Tomato

2 - 4
Servings

9
Ingredients

10
Minutes

**~1.5 lbs /
~700g**
Weight

Vegan

Vegetarian

No Burner

Dairy Free

Low Water

Ingredients	US	Metrics
1. Olive Oil	1/2 C	50 g
2. Vinegar, your fav	1/4 C	25 g
3. Salt	1/2 tsp	2 g
4. Black pepper	1/2 tsp	2 g
5. Dijon mustard packets	2	20 g
6. Kale	1 bunch	1 bunch
7. Carrot	1	1
8. Shallot	1	1
9. Baby tomatoes	8 oz	200 g

Steps

* NO BURNER *

1. CHOP kale, carrot, shallot, tomatoes
2. + vinegar to veggies. MIX
3. + oil, dijon mustard, salt, black pepper
4. MIX
5. SIT for 5 min
   EAT

Notes/Additions
*Did you know that? Kale was originally only used as
decoration on plates and in planter boxes. Now
people enjoy over 10 varieties in many types of dishes.
Now you know!*

Pack it out!

German Potato Salad

2 – 4
Servings

9
Ingredients

25
Minutes

**~4 lbs /
~1.8 kg**
Weight

Vegan

Vegetarian

Dairy Free

High Calorie

Ingredients	US	Metrics
1. Water	32 oz	1 L
2. Red potatoes	6-8	6-8
3. Salt	1-2 tsp	8 g
4. Green beans, fresh	8 oz	225 g
5. Baby tomatoes	6 oz	170 g
6. Shallot	2	2
7. Stone ground mustard	1/4 C	25 g
8. Apple cider vinegar	1/4 C	25 g
9. Black pepper	1/2 tsp	2 g

Steps

1. CHOP potatoes
2. **TURN ON BURNER: High heat**
3. + water, potatoes, salt
4. BOIL until soft. DRAIN
5. CHOP green beans, tomatoes, shallots
6. + vegetables, mustard, vinegar, black pepper
7. MIX. MIX
8. + salt to taste
EAT

Notes/Additions
*Did you know that? Only one state in the US does not
have either a national park or national monument. It is
actually the country's first state, Delaware.
Now you know!*

Pack it out!

Moroccan Couscous

2 – 4
Servings

8
Ingredients

10
Minutes

**~2.2 lbs /
~1 kg**
Weight

Vegan

Vegetarian

Dairy Free

Ingredients

		US	Metrics
1.	Water	20 oz	600 ml
2.	Couscous, instant	2 box/11.6 oz	2 box/320 g
3.	Olive oil	2 TB	25 g
4.	Dried apricots	1/2 C	50 g
5.	Almonds	1/2 C	50 g
6.	Salt	1 tsp	5 g
7.	Black pepper	1/2 tsp	2 g
8.	Mint	1/4 C	15 g

Steps

1. **TURN ON BURNER: High heat**
2. BOIL WATER
3. + cous cous. FOLLOW pkg instructions
4. CHOP apricots, almonds, mint
5. when couscous DONE, + olive oil, apricots, almonds, salt, black pepper, mint
6. MIX
EAT

Notes/Additions
*Did you know that? Couscous is actually not a grain, but a pasta. Just water and flour.
Now you know!*

Pack it out!

Mediterranean Tuna

Tested by
Belosho

2
Servings

8
Ingredients

15
Minutes

**~2.2 lbs /
~1kg**
Weight

Ingredients	US	Metrics
1. Tuna	10 oz	285 g
2. Olives	4 oz	115 g
3. Capers	2 TB	20 g
4. Green beans, fresh	8 oz	225 g
5. Baby tomatoes	8 oz	225 g
6. Lemon	1	1
7. Olive oil	1/4 C	50 g
8. Black pepper	1/2 tsp	2 g

Low Water

Dairy Free

No Burner

High Calorie

Steps

* NO BURNER *

1. CHOP green beans, tomatoes
2. + tuna, olives, green beans, tomatoes, lemon juice, olive oil, black pepper
3. MIX. SIT for 5 min
EAT

Notes/Additions
Did you know that? You can visit two National Parks in a day if you visit Yellowstone and Grand Teton National Parks. They are just 10 miles apart in northern Wyoming.
Now you know!

Pack it out!

Notes

Dinner

**Tom Yum
Noodle Bowl**
Thunder Creek
North Cascades NP, WA

**Garlic Chicken,
Artichokes &
Mashed Potatoes**
Mt Rainier, WA

**Turkey Day
Stuffing Bowl**
Lake Union, WA

Jambalaya
Seattle, WA

Tom Yum Noodle Bowl

Special

2 – 4
Servings

10
Ingredients

25
Minutes

**~5 lbs /
~2.2 kg**
Weight

Vegan

Vegetarian

Dairy Free

Ingredients	US	Metrics
1. Onion	1	1
2. Baby bok choy	2-3	2-3
3. Baby corn	1 can	1 can
4. Ginger	1 finger	1 finger
5. Thai curry paste	2 TB	30 g
6. Coconut milk powder	3 TB	20 g
7. Fish sauce or salt	2 TB or 1 tsp	30 g or 5 g
8. Rice noodles	2 bunch / 7 oz	200 g
9. Water	32 oz	1 L
10. Lime	1	1

Steps

1. **TURN ON BURNER: High heat**
2. + water, noodles. BOIL
3. BOIL until almost done
5. CHOP onion, bok choy, ginger, WEDGE limes
6. OPEN can baby corn
7. + onion, ginger baby corn, fish sauce, curry paste, coconut powder, water
8. STIR. BOIL. 5 min
9. + bok choy. COOK 1-2 min
10. GARNISH w/lime wedges
EAT

Notes/Additions

This is a great starting point. You can always mix it up with other veggies, meats and nuts that are available.

Pack it out!

Garlic Chicken w/ Artichokes, Mashed Potatoes

2 - 4
Servings

9
Ingredients

15
Minutes

~3.3 lbs / ~1.5 kg
Weight

High Calorie

Ingredients

	Ingredients	US	Metrics
1.	Olive oil	2 TB	25 g
2.	Shallot	2	2
3.	Garlic	3 clvs	3 clvs
4.	Artichoke hearts	1 can	400 g
5.	Canned chicken	12.5 oz	354 g
6.	Instant mashed potatoes	1 pkg / 4 oz	113 g
7.	Water	16 oz	475 ml
8.	Lemon	1	1
9.	Salt	1 tsp	5 g

Steps

1. CHOP shallot, garlic
2. OPEN cans
3. **TURN ON BURNER: Med heat**
4. + olive oil, shallot, garlic, salt
5. COOK 2 min
6. + artichoke hearts, chicken water
7. SIMMER 3-5 min
8. + instant potatoes
9. COOK by package instructions.
10. GARNISH with lemon wedge
EAT

Notes/Additions

Did you know that? Artichokes are a member of the thistle family and can produce over 20 artichokes per year.
Now you know!

Pack it out!

Turkey Day Stuffing Bowl

2 – 4
Servings

8
Ingredients

25
Minutes

**~4 lbs /
~1.8 kg**
Weight

Dairy Free

High Calorie

Ingredients

	US	Metrics
1. Water	24 oz	700 ml
2. Stuffing mix	2 pkg / 12 oz	340 g
3. Oil	2 TB	25 g
4. Gravy mix, turkey	1 pkg / .87 oz	24 g
5. Packaged chicken or	10 oz / 1 lb	454 g
Field Roast Celebration		
6. Green beans, fresh	8 oz	225 g
7. Cranberries, dried	1/4 C	25 g
8. Salt	1 tsp	5 g

Steps

1. CHOP field roast, green beans
2. **TURN ON BURNER: High heat**
3. + oil, chicken/field roast, cranberries, beans, salt
4. COOK 2-3 min until cooked
5. + water, stuffing mix, gravy mix
6. STIR, BOIL.
7. TURN OFF BURNER
8. COVER. SIT re package instructions
9. FLUFF
EAT

Notes/Additions
*Did you know that? Everyone needs a good fluff from
time to time.
Now you know!*

Pack it out!

Jambalaya

2 - 4
Servings

10
Ingredients

25
Minutes

**~3.7 lbs /
~1.7 kg**
Weight

High Calorie

Dairy Free

Ingredients

Ingredients	US	Metrics
1. Olive oil	2 TB	25 g
2. Shallot	1	1
3. Green bell pepper	1	1
4. Celery	2 stalks	2 stalks
5. Garlic	2 clvs	2 clvs
6. Chicken sausage, precooked	12 oz	340 g
7. Tomato paste	2 TB	30 g
8. Old Bay/creole seasoning	2 TB	30 g
9. Instant rice	2 C	350 g
10. Water	16 oz	475 ml

Steps

1. CHOP shallot, bell pepper, celery, garlic, sausage
2. **TURN ON BURNER: Med heat**
3. + olive oil, sausage
4. COOK 2-3 min
5. + onion, bell pepper, celery
6. COOK 2-3 min
7. + tomato paste, creole seasoning
8. STIR. COOK 1 min
9. + water. BOIL
10. + rice. STIR. COVER
11. TURN OFF BURNER. SIT 10 min
12. FLUFF

EAT

Notes/Additions

Did you know that? An adult flamingo's legs can be 30-50 inches long, which is longer than its entire body. Now you know!

Pack it out!

Notes

Chocolate Marshmallow Fondue
Seward Park, WA

Caramelized Banana Nilla Wafer Bowl
Deming, WA

Fresh Apple Pear Crisp
Clear Creek - NCNP, WA

Blueberry Lemon Rice Crispy Treat Bowl
Sedona, WA

Chocolate Marshmallow Fondue with Seasonal Fruit

4-8
Servings

5
Ingredients

10
Minutes

~2.5 lbs / ~750 g
Weight

Low Water

Vegetarian

High Calorie

Ingredients	US	Metrics
1. Marshmallows	3 oz	100 g
2. Chocolate chips	12 oz	340 g
3. Fruit 1	1	1
4. Fruit 2	2	2
5. Fruit 3	6 oz	100 g

Steps

1. CUT fruit into pieces/wedges
2. WHITTLE campy fondue sticks
3. **TURN ON BURNER: Low heat**
4. + chocolate. STIR. MELT
5. + marshmellows. STIR. MELT
6. **TURN OFF BURNER**
I DIP, YOU DIP, WE DIP

Notes/Additions

Great dessert for sharing. Make your own fondue sticks with available twigs...but hey, don't chop down a tree.

Pack it out!

Caramelized Banana Nilla Wafer Bowl

2 - 4
Servings

5
Ingredients

10
Minutes

**~2.2 lbs /
~1 kg**
Weight

Low Water

Vegetarian

Dairy Free

High Calorie

Ingredients	US	Metrics
1. Banana	2	2
2. Brown sugar	1/2 C	95 g
3. Water	2 oz	60 ml
4. Nilla Wafer, crushed	2 C	220 g
5. Nuts, your choice	1/2 C	50 g

Steps

1. CUT bananas into coins
2. CHOP nuts & Nilla Wafers
3. **TURN ON BURNER: Med heat**
4. + brown sugar, water
5. SIMMER for 1 min
6. + bananas
7. SIMMER on LOW 2-4 min until coated
8. + Nilla Wafers to serving bowl
9. POUR over banana mixture
10. + nuts
EAT

Notes/Additions
Great with a nip of whiskey or rum!

MONT
BOCA

Pack it out!

Fresh Apple Pear Crisp

4
Servings

9
Ingredients

25
Minutes

**~2 lbs /
~900 g**
Weight

Vegan

Vegetarian

Low Water

High Calorie

Dairy Free

Ingredients	US	Metrics
1. Apple variety 1	1	1
2. Apple variety 2	1	1
3. Pear variety 1	1	1
4. Pear variety 2	1	1
5. Sugar	2-4 TB	50 g
6. Cinnamon	1 tsp	2 g
7. Water	8 oz	230 ml
8. Apple cider vinegar	2 tsp	10 g
9. Granola, your fav	2 C	300 g

Steps

1. CHOP small apples, pears into dice-sized pieces
2. **TURN ON BURNER: Med heat**
3. + fruit, sugar, cinnamon, water
4. STIR. COOK 12-15 min until soft
5. + apple cider vinegar. STIR
6. + granola on top
EAT

Notes/Additions

*Need some whipped cream? Pack a small vanilla
yogurt! Also great with nuts or raisins!*

Pack it out!

Blueberry Lemon Rice Crispy Bowl

2 - 4
Servings

7
Ingredients

10
Minutes

**~2 lbs /
~1 kg**
Weight

Dairy Free

Vegetarian

Low Water

Ingredients

Ingredients	US	Metrics
1. Oil	3 TB	40 g
2. Marshmallows	4 oz	150 g
3. Water	2 oz	60 g
4. Rice Crispy cereal	4 C	400 g
5. Blueberries	6 oz	170 g
6. Lemon	1	1
7. Banana chips	1/4 C	25 g

Steps

1. **TURN ON BURNER: Med heat**
2. + oil, marshmallow, water
3. STIR. COOK until melted
4. **TURN OFF BURNER**
5. + blueberries, banana chips, rice crispies
6. STIR
7. SQUEEZE lemon over mix
EAT

Notes/Additions

*Did you know that? Cereal originated at spas in Battle Creek, Michigan, where it quickly gained popularity as a "health food".
Now you know!*

Pack it out!

Notes

MONT
I BOCA

Trail-gate

Nacho y Nachos
Artist Point
Bellingham, WA

**Burst Tomato
Goat Cheese Dip**
Joshua Tree NP, CA

**Cheesy German
Sausage Dip w Mustard**
Hood Canal, WA

**Honey Sriracha
Popcorn**
Leschi, WA

Nacho y Nachos

2 - 4
Servings

7
Ingredients

10
Minutes

**~2.8 lbs /
~1.2 g**
Weight

`High Calorie`

`Vegetarian`

`Low Water`

Ingredients

	Ingredients	US	Metrics
1.	Shallot	2	2
2.	Jalepeno	1	1
3.	Salsa pack	16 oz	450 g
4.	Velveeta cheese	16 oz	450 g
5.	Lime	1	1
6.	Cilantro	1 bunch	1 bunch
7.	Tortilla chips	1 lg bag	1 lg bag

Steps

1. CHOP jalapeno, shallot, cilantro
2. **TURN ON BURNER: Med heat**
3. COOK shallot, jalapeno
4. + Velveeta, salsa pack
5. COOK 3-5 min until cheese melts
6. + lime juice, cilantro
7. STIR STIR
I DIP, YOU DIP, WE DIP

Notes/Additions
Did you know that?
*Velveeta was invented in 1918 by Emil Frey of the
Monroe Cheese Company in Monroe, New York.
Now you know!*

MONT
Y BOCA

Pack it out!

Goat Cheese Dip w/ Burst Tomatoes

Tested by
Chef Corso

2 – 4
Servings

9
Ingredients

10
Minutes

**~3 lbs /
~1.5 kg**
Weight

`Low Water`

`Vegetarian`

`High Calorie`

Ingredients

Ingredients	US	Metrics
1. Olive oil	1 TB	14 g
2. Garlic	2 clvs	2 clvs
3. Baby tomatoes	10.5 oz	300 g
4. Oregano, dried	1 tsp	2 g
5. Chili flake	1 tsp	2 g
6. Salt	1 tsp	5 g
7. Goat cheese	16 oz	450 g
8. Bread, your fav	1 loaf	1 loaf
9. Crackers, your fav	1 pkg	1 loaf

Steps

1. CHOP garlic
2. **TURN ON BURNER: Med heat**
3. + oil, garlic, tomatoes, oregano, chili flake, salt
4. **COOK 2-3 min until burst. STIR**
5. **BURNER: Low heat**
6. + goat cheese, STIR, MELT
I DIP, YOU DIP, WE DIP

Notes/Additions

Did you know that? California is home to the world's largest tree, General Sherman Tree, in Sequoia National Park
Now you know!

MONT
YBOCA

Pack it out!

Cheesy German Sausage & Mustard Dip

4-6
Servings

9
Ingredients

20
Minutes

~ 2.6 lbs / ~1.2 kg
Weight

`High Calorie`

`Low Water`

Ingredients	US	Metrics
1. Shallot	2	2
2. Garlic	2 clvs	2 clvs
3. Olive oil	2 TB	25 g
4. German sausage, precooked	12 oz	250 g
5. Swiss/Gueyre cheese	8 oz	225 g
6. Stone ground mustard	1/4 C	60 g
7. Apple cider vinegar	2 TB	25 g
8. Pretzels, your fav	16 oz	450 g
9. Whole grain crackers, your fav	1 box	1 box

Steps

1. CHOP shallot, garlic, sausage, cheese
2. **TURN ON BURER: Med heat**
3. + oil, shallot, garlic, sausage
4. COOK 3-5 min. STIR
5. + cheese
6. STIR. MELT (be patient...it will happen)
7. + mustard, vinegar
8. STIR. COOK 1 min
I DIP, YOU DIP, WE DIP

Notes/Additions
Did you know that? Some female sharks use sperm from multiple males to reproduce, resulting in pups from the same pregnancy being half-siblings.
Now you know!

Pack it out!

Honey Sriracha Popcorn

4 - 6
Servings

5
Ingredients

10
Minutes

**~.5 lbs /
~200 g**
Weight

Vegan

Vegetarian

Dairy Free

Low Water

Ingredients

		US	Metrics
1.	Oil	3 TB	40 g
2.	Popcorn	2 oz	55 g
3.	Salt	1 tsp	5 g
4.	Sriracha	1 TB	15 g
5.	Honey packets	2	2

Steps

1. **TURN BURNER ON: High heat**
2. + oil & 3 kernels
3. WAIT for kernels to pop!
4. + all kernels, salt
5. MOVE QUICK. TOSS. TOSS. COVER. TOSS
6. when done popping, + sriracha, honey
7. TOSS
EAT

Notes/Additions
*Make sure to cover while you toss or you will get
splattered with oil! No bueno.*

Pack it out!

Notes

Join the MONTyBOCA Community and become a Recipe Tester!

What does that mean?

Receive a NEW recipe from Chef Corso.
Take it outside.
Test it.
Take a couple photos.
Share feedback.

**Chef Corso edits and shares
with the whole community!**

www.montyboca.com/recipe-tester

Take Me Camping Mission:
plain and simple, we just want to
encourage people to go camping.
That's it.

This may sound overly simple but there's
a pretty good reason why we keep our
mission this direct.

We strongly believe that a lot of great
things occur when people go camping,

Need a campsite?
Need some new gear?
Need some travel tips?

Check out:
www.takemecamping.org

Follow along:
Instagram: @montyboca
YouTube: Chef Corso
Pinterest: MONTyBOCA

Chef Corso Bio in back
Photography Credit:
MONTyBOCA, Sattva Photography, Roland Mott
Logo & formatting credit: Ronald Viernes

ISBN number: 978-1-7341902-0-5

First (Origin) Edition

Get outside. Eat well. Share the tasty experience
#elevateyourmeals
bocaboca

Chef Corso Bio

Chef Corso likes to eat and go outside. He's also a classically trained chef - training in Napa Valley and Northern Italy. On his treks, he noticed the food options were pretty bad - dry, salty, expensive, and out of a bag. He started testing simple recipes, using fresh ingredients, with the hiker/camper in mind.
The results were amazing! Tasty food that complimented the beautiful vista like nothing he had experienced before. He wanted to share these recipes as he believes everyone should eat well on their adventures outside - MONTyBOCA can show you how.

Get outside. Eat well. Share the experience.

MONTyBOCA is headquartered in Seattle, WA.
All recipes are trail-tested across the continent.

bocaboca